CHIEF JOSEPH
and his People

In the 1860s it was government policy in the United States to deprive the Indians of their land and their freedom, and to concentrate them on reservations where the earth was often barren, and movement restricted. Chief Joseph and his tribe, the Nez Percés, attempted to resist this displacement, non-violently at first, but when eventually blood was shed, Chief Joseph led the entire tribe over 1300 miles of rugged terrain, fighting all the way. Their aim was Canada and safety, but they were outnumbered, and their brave struggle ended in defeat a mere 40 miles from the border.

CHIEF JOSEPH
and his People

WILLIAM RAYNER

Collins

To John and Irene Izod

William Collins Sons & Co Ltd
London · Glasgow · Sydney · Auckland
Toronto · Johannesburg

First published 1979
© William Rayner 1979
ISBN 0 00 195124 6
Made and printed in Great Britain by
William Collins Sons & Co Ltd Glasgow

Diary of Events

1805	First known encounter between white men and members of the Nez Percé tribe. The Indians offer friendship and help to the Lewis and Clark Expedition when it passes through their territory.
1860	Gold strikes at Orofino, followed by other strikes, bring prospectors and settlers flocking to North West.
1863	Upper Nez Percés accept treaty which entails them settling on reservation at Lapwai. Lower Nez Percés, under Old Joseph, reject the treaty and continue their free, roving life.
1869	Transcontinental Union Pacific Railway completed.
1870	The enormous slaughter of the buffalo herds begins.
1871	Old Joseph dies. His son, Chief Joseph, assumes leadership of the Lower Nez Percés.
1872	U.S. government officials visit Joseph and urge him to give up his ancestral lands, centred on the Wallowa Valley. Joseph counters by appealing directly to Ulysses Grant, President of the United States.
1873	President Grant rules in favour of Chief Joseph, and orders the Wallowa Valley to be closed to further white settlement.
1875	Under pressure from white interests, President Grant reverses his decision and re-opens the Wallowa country to white settlement.
1876	Outrages and clashes mount between white men and Nez Percés. A brother of Chief Joseph is killed by a white settler.

1876	U.S. Army campaign mounted to pacify, disarm and force on to reservations the powerful Sioux and Northern Cheyenne occupying the Powder River country. Led by Crazy Horse and Sitting Bull, the Indians defeat the U.S. forces at the battle of the Little Big Horn (June 25th). General Custer and his column of 7th Cavalry wiped out. Strong U.S. punitive expeditions dispatched. Indians scattered and harried over following months.
1876	Government Commission set up to decide whether Joseph and his people should be removed forcibly to a reservation.
1877	Commission rules that Joseph and the Nez Percés must go on to the Lapwai reservation by 14th May. Joseph accepts but some of his young men decide to strike back. Several white settlers killed. Chief Joseph reluctantly assumes military command.
16th May	Column of regular troops under Colonel Perry ordered to punish the Nez Percés and force them on to the reservation. Chief Joseph ambushes Perry's column at White Bird canyon and routs it.
11th June	General Howard and larger column attack Joseph's camp on the Clearwater River. After a fierce fight, Joseph effects a skilful withdrawal. Leads his people over the Lolo Trail into Montana.
28th July	Joseph foils the attempt of Captain Rawn's detachment to block his way with a barricade.
Early August	Joseph leads his people down into the Big Hole country. Unknown to him, he is being pursued by yet another army column, under Colonel Gibbon.
9th August	Gibbon launches surprise dawn attack on Nez Percé encampment. Joseph leads furious counter-attack.

Gibbon's men cornered and only saved by approach of General Howard's column. Nez Percés retreat.

Early September
Joseph leads his people into Yellowstone country. He is pursued by yet another column, under Colonel Sturgis and attacked at Canyon Creek. Joseph makes a clever fighting withdrawal. The Nez Percés head for sanctuary in Canada.

23rd September
The Nez Percés strike the Missouri at Cow Island and cross the river.

29th September
The Nez Percés reach the area of the Bear Paw and Little Rocky Mountains, only thirty miles from Canada. Joseph decides to risk a day's rest for his exhausted people.

30th September
The Nez Percés surprised and attacked by advance column arriving from East under command of Colonel Miles. The Nez Percés are pinned down.

3rd October
General Howard's column arrives to reinforce Miles's troops. Chief Joseph attends meeting to discuss surrender terms. That night White Bird's band breaks out and reaches Canada, where it joins the Sioux refugees under Sitting Bull.

4th October
Chief Joseph surrenders, on terms. The agreement is not kept by U.S. officials. The Nez Percés are shipped to Fort Leavenworth, Kansas, and later to the Salt Fork of the Arkansas River. They sicken.

1885
Most of Nez Percé survivors allowed to rejoin their fellow tribesmen at Lapwai. Permission refused to Chief Joseph and some other warriors. They are sent instead to Colville Reservation, Washington.

1904
Chief Joseph dies, still in exile from his people.

"The whites told only one side. Told it to please themselves. Told much that is not true. Only his own best deeds, only the worst deeds of the Indians, has the white man told."

Yellow Wolf (Nez Percé) 1880

CHIEF JOSEPH
and his People

This is the story of the Lower Nez Percés, a tribe of North American Indians only a few hundred strong, who were driven to defend themselves against the inroads of white settlers, and the demands made by the United States government of the time. The struggle of the Nez Percés took place in 1877, but it is not an event that should be seen in isolation. It echoes earlier struggles on the part of the Indians, and may serve to show the fate that overtook them all. Though many Indian tribes had travelled down the same tragic road, there was reserved for the Nez Percés the sombre distinction of being the last of all the tribes in the north to put up a fight for their freedom. Their struggle was also distinguished by its outstanding heroism, and by the presence amongst them of Chief Joseph, a leader of great wisdom and nobility, who was to prove himself amongst the most moving of all speakers in defence of the Indian way of life. Chief Joseph's voice rings down the years, and his opinions, unheeded by the white men of his time, now seem to bear an important message for the modern world.

In order to see Chief Joseph and his people in context, we must try, first of all, to get a general picture of the North American Indians, who might fairly be described as the original owners of America. Certainly, they had been living there for many centuries before the white man arrived. Their ancestors seem to have come, at different times, across the land bridge that once existed between Asia and Alaska. From there, they spread throughout the continent, and by the time the white man was in a position to observe them, they were well established in every sort of region, including the most desolate and inhospitable. It is not surprising that Indian societies, scattered across these huge expanses, should have developed differences in life-style, though as we shall see, they also had much in common.

More than five hundred distinct Indian languages were spoken in the territory that is now the United States, and there were an even greater number of tribes in existence. It was not just a matter of differences of language: different tribes had worked out different ways of governing themselves. Some, like the Indians on the eastern seaboard, seem to have had hereditary chiefs whom the early English settlers called "kings". Others, like the famous Iroquois who lived in what is now New York State, settled for a more democratic arrangement. Amongst them, the business of government was carried on by councils of mature men, but interestingly, membership of these councils was decided by the important women of the tribe, who had powers not only of appointment but also of dismissal. This system was arranged so that both sexes played an important role, with women finally predominant. Life was very different among the Natchez tribe which lived near the Mississippi delta. Natchez society was divided into several sharply defined classes, all of them ruled over by an absolute monarch known as the Great Sun, who also acted as high-priest. The Natchez are only mentioned here to show the extreme variations it was possible to find amongst the Indian tribes. More typical was the kind of arrangement found amongst such farming tribes of the South West as the Pima or Papago. These people were very democratic, governing themselves by means of a council of elders who would elect one of their number as leader when the need arose. These leaders were far from being kings or despots. Tribal decisions still depended on the unanimous agreement of the council, and the job of the leader was to try to bring them to one mind, and act as the "voice" of the assembly. Most Indian tribes, the Nez Percés among them, followed this pattern of democratic debate. Their chiefs were men of prestige and influence rather than dictators.

The family was also of great importance to the Indian way of life, and the ties of blood were widely recognized amongst them. It was what we call the "extended" type of family, involving a considerable number of kinsfolk who would be more closely knitted and more dependent on each other than is the case in modern Western society. In some tribes, it was the custom when a couple married for the wife to go and live with her husband's kin, but among other tribes, it was the husband who would join the family group of his wife. The idea of two young people setting up on their own, perhaps far away from any other members of their kinsfolk, was alien to tribal life, and would have had no attraction to Indians. The position of

children was different amongst them, too. Children called not only their own parents "Father" and "Mother", but various other relatives as well. This meant that if a child lost its real parents, either by divorce or death, there were other "parents" at hand to care for it. An Indian child had the confidence of belonging to a large and practically indestructible family unit.

Right from the beginning, Indian ways of looking at the world seem to have puzzled and alarmed the white settlers of America. To take a crucial example, Indian views on the ownership of land were very different from those of Europeans. Indians did not think of land as property that could be held by an individual and his heirs forever. Land was a tribal asset with them, and they made their arrangements about it accordingly. Throughout the nineteenth century, Indians acting as spokesmen for tribes threatened with dispossession tried to explain to white Commissioners the depth of their feeling for the land, and for nature in general. As we shall see, Chief Joseph made the attempt. His speech was admired in some quarters for its eloquence, but the ideas he put forward stood no chance of being taken seriously. There was too great a gulf between the views of the Indian and the white man for that to happen. Ironically, the Indian was regarded then as a squanderer of natural resources because he did nothing to wring quick money from them. It was not only inevitable, it was also *right* that he be swept aside so that the land could be forced to give up its treasures. It was sincerely felt that the Indian had condemned

Nez Percé child in his costume of furs, beads, shells and quills

13

himself by his lack of enterprise, and it is true that Indians did not share the appetite for sudden wealth which was the driving force among white men. The Indian attitude towards the natural world was based on love rather than aggression. White men had – and many still have – a tendency to treat nature first as an enemy to be defeated, and then as a victim to be exploited. This was not the Indian way. Amongst them, young people were brought up to show respect for the natural order of things. Their aim must not be to abuse or disrupt that order but to put themselves in harmony with it. It was thought that a man could only avoid disaster by striving to understand the ways of nature as far as possible, and where that was beyond him, by showing reverence towards its mysteries. They carried with them a deep sense of what Black Elk of the Sioux called "the strangeness and beauty of the world".

An Indian felt himself to be part of nature, not an enemy to it. That was the essential difference. In fact, Indians believed that a man's powers were drawn directly from nature, which the Indians looked at with a mystical eye, seeing spiritual forces at work everywhere within it, in the wind, the stars, the lightning, the mountains, and the animal creation. Indians, convinced of the power of the spiritual forces that underlay the world of nature, tried to gain enlightenment from them. In many tribes, it was the custom for young men to set out alone into the mountains in order to search for the spirits that might help them. Often they would fast for days and inflict deliberate pain and hardship on themselves, believing this was the way to break down the barrier between themselves and the spirit world. What they were seeking on such quests was a personal revelation which came to them in dreams or waking visions, often assuming the shape of a spirit animal. The kind of revelation they received would influence them for the rest of their life. Such visions were thought to give men a variety of powers, making one a good hunter, another an expert healer, a third an outstanding warrior, a fourth a magician or seer. Those people who could most freely gain access to the world of spirits were thought to merit great respect, and often rose to positions of influence among the Indians. Men like Crazy Horse or Sitting Bull remain famous today as war-chiefs; what is not so well known is that both of them were "medicine-men", visionaries whose advanced spiritual powers were thought to make them superior in wisdom and judgement, which in turn allowed them to lead others successfully in battle.

In most Indian societies, war held an honoured place. War, with its demands on the courage and physical strength of a man, was seen as a school of spiritual discipline. Danger and hardship – as in the quest for visions – strengthened the soul. Able warriors were held in great esteem, and young men strove hard to win a reputation for courage and astuteness in the raids that Indian tribes used to mount against each other. The feathers they wore in their hair were military decorations, awarded by fellow tribesmen as the visible sign of a man's prowess. War amongst them seems to have been regarded as a fierce, exciting ritual which gave a man the chance to prove himself, and develop his spiritual powers. In their raids, killing was not itself the main object of the exercise. A man gained honour by actually going up to an enemy and striking him, not by shooting him from a safe distance. This practice, called "counting *coup*", makes clear how very different were Indian ideas of fighting from those held by white men. Daring brought honour, and honour was the important thing for an Indian, in peace as well as war. To take another example, an Indian did not gain status because of the large number of horses he had accumulated, but because he had put himself in a position where he could give many horses away. He achieved honour by a display of generosity, choosing spiritual over material wealth. This kind of thinking was absolutely contrary to the climate of opinion in white society, where people were brought up to believe that their best chance of claiming the respect of others was by amassing unusually large amounts of money.

The high regard Indians felt for courage and spiritual excellence had also led them to adopt darker practices which must be touched on here because they appear so often, and are given such weight, in the white man's denunciations of Indian savagery. Descriptions of the torture of prisoners, and the scalping of dead enemies, have always loomed large in white accounts of Indian customs. What the settlers failed to grasp was that, to the Indian, torture was not pursued out of simple cruelty. They engaged in torture because they had carried their beliefs about spiritual strength through to a perverse extreme. Torture was a dreadful contest in which the captive was challenged to show his spiritual power by his ability to ignore pain. It must be remembered in this context that Indian warriors regularly undertook self-torture at public religious occasions such as the Sun Dance. These remarks are made, not to excuse torture, but to show how it fitted into the Indian system of values.

As for scalping, this, too, had a religious meaning among Indians, who mutilated enemy dead in this and other ways because they were under the impression that the soul of a dead man was influenced by the state of his corpse. A damaged corpse meant a feeble soul, unable to harm its enemies among the living. The scalp was particularly important in this respect. Indians believed they could restore spiritual strength and integrity to the soul of one of their own dead by supplying him with another scalp, taken from an enemy. Thus, scalping was not to do with vengeance or prestige, but with putting the dead together again. Indian reasoning here may seem very odd to us, not to say grotesque, but at least we can see that cruelty was not practised for its own sake. It rested on a foundation of spiritual belief. Scalping had no such meanings for white men, but many pioneers adopted the practice and scalped any Indians they killed as a matter of retaliation. Happily, the Nez Percés were one of the few tribes who do not seem to have indulged in these unnerving practices, at least during the period when we shall be considering them.

From as early as the seventeenth century, white men had begun to move westward and this invariably meant invading territory held by Indians. Wherever dubious land transfers could not be arranged by treaty, there was war. Often the Indians defended their country stubbornly, but the truth was that the white man, usually superior in numbers and always in weapons, could not be withstood for ever. Tribe after tribe was defeated and removed from its ancestral lands. In addition to guns and whisky, the white man brought with him new diseases against which the Indians had little resistance. They found themselves devastated by epidemics of measles, cholera, tuberculosis, and above all, smallpox. The Mandan tribe provides an extreme example of the ravages caused by the new diseases. Formerly the Mandan had been a thriving tribe of hunters and farmers living on the banks of the Missouri, but by the mid-nineteenth century repeated epidemics of smallpox had practically wiped them out.

If the white man brought much sadness and disruption to the Indians, he also unwittingly presented them with a great gift. Before the white man arrived in America, the only beast of burden among the Indians was the dog. When they set out on the fall-hunt of the buffalo, it was the dog which dragged the wooden framework carrying their household possessions and even their small children. Hunting was done on foot. The early Spanish explorers, pushing up from Mexico, astonished and struck fear into the *pueblo* Indians by appearing on the backs of great beasts, the like of which no Indian had ever seen before. The horse had made its first appearance in America!

Gradually, the Indians got hold of horses themselves,

though it was a slow process. Not until the end of the seventeenth century did the horse reach the Utes, a mountain tribe living in Colorado, and it was not adopted by the Indians of the northern plains until later still. Wherever the horse made its appearance, it changed the Indian way of life. The changes were sometimes spectacular. For instance, until about 1740 both the Sioux and the Cheyenne had been farmers and hunters in the northern woodlands. Once the horse reached them, they launched out into a new life on the great plains. They became nomads, following the buffalo herds and taking from them all the necessities of life. Among "horse-nations" such as these, the Indian characteristics of courage, endurance and vision were brought to a high pitch.

The horse seems to have reached the Nez Percés and the other tribes of the north-west plateaux slightly earlier than it appeared among the Sioux, but the change it made in their way of life was by no means so great. This was because of the country in which these tribes lived. The terrain was rugged, with high, broken tablelands, out of which thrust many ranges of hills and mountains, their sides often girdled with timber. Rainfall was low and sage-brush grew in the more arid regions, though there was plenty of water in the streams flowing down from the mountains. Some rivers ran from high lakes down narrow green valleys, others surged at the foot of immense canyons that their waters had cut in the rock. It was a land of jumbled ridges, lakes, canyons, waterfalls, hot springs – a very different sort of country from the level plains with their

overleaf: this area, Joseph's Canyon, is typical of the rugged tribal lands of the Nez Percés

vast horizons, and it lacked the immense herds of buffalo found there. The men of the plateaux hunted such game as deer, elk, mountain-sheep and jackrabbits. They also fished the rivers, the most prized catch being trout and salmon, which they preserved by smoking. The nature of the country did not encourage attempts at farming. Instead, the women gathered wild fruits and berries, and dug for edible roots. In winter, these peoples had traditionally donned cloaks, often of rabbit fur, and dug themselves pithouses roofed with branches and mats to keep out the cold.

When they adopted the horse, Indians such as the Nez Percés also took over a style of dress borrowed from the horse-nations, as well as some of their hunting techniques. They began to live in the tepee or hidetent most commonly associated with the nomads of the plains. Now that they were mounted, Nez Percé hunting parties were able to make the long arduous journey across the Rocky Mountains each year to take part in the *illahu* – the fall-hunt of the buffalo. They went to the famous hunting ground called the Powder River Country which was held by the Sioux, with whom they seem to have been on good terms, and came trekking back over the mountains, their horses loaded with meat and hides that would help their people through the hard northern winter.

After the end of the War Between The States in 1865, pressure mounted rapidly on the remaining free Indian tribes, particularly the nomads of the plains. The United States government decided to remove them all to reservations, dismount and disarm them and convert them to Christianity. Any tribes that proved defiant were to be systematically "punished" by the army until they changed their minds. This policy was vigorously pursued by men such as General Custer.

Other events at this time were also threatening the Plains Indians. Railways were being pushed across the continent, the first of them, the Union Pacific, being completed in 1869. Not only did the railways bring hordes of new settlers, they also impeded the yearly migrations of the buffalo, on which the Indians depended. Railways meant that goods could be transported in bulk to the cities of the East and white settlers were not slow to take advantage of the fact. They realized there was quick money to be made by supplying the cities of America and Europe with buffalo "robes", for which there was a ready demand. There followed an incredible slaughter of the buffalo. Each year from about 1870 more than a million buffalo were shot. Only their hides were taken, the carcases being left to rot on the plains. This carnage was carried on by white hunters out of a simple desire for profit, but its implications for the Indians were well understood at government level, and the slaughter was encouraged for that reason. General Sheridan stated that the hunters "should kill, skin and sell unhindered until the buffalo is exterminated, as this is the only way to bring lasting peace and allow civilization to advance".

The Plains Indians fought back against these devastating blows, but by the mid 1870s the buffalo had

overleaf:
Nez Percé hunting parties travelled across the Rocky Mountains each year to take part in the autumn buffalo-hunt

23

vanished from the southern ranges, and the tribes who lived there, such as the Kiowas and the Comanches, had been defeated. Their survivors, broken and starving, were committed to reservations. Only in the north was there still resistance. The powerful Sioux confederacy still claimed the rich hunting grounds of the Powder River. This was hardly surprising since they had signed a treaty with the United States government only eight years before which guaranteed Sioux ownership of this land "forever". By 1876, the government had revised its opinion. Notwithstanding the treaty, the Sioux had to be removed from the Powder River Country and from their sacred mountains, the Black Hills, where gold had been found. When the Sioux ignored orders to come in, troops were sent against them. The Sioux war-chiefs, Crazy Horse and Sitting Bull, led their people to a famous victory at the battle of the Little Big Horn, where they wiped out General Custer and his column of Seventh Cavalry, but this victory only served to hasten their end. White people in the United States were outraged at the news; the press cried out for vengeance, and more and more columns of troops were sent to harry the now scattered Sioux bands. One by one, they were forced to surrender. Only Sitting Bull escaped the common fate by leading his band across the border into Canada. The rest of the Sioux were disarmed and sent as captives to a reservation on the Missouri, in an area that was strange to them.

After the collapse of Sioux resistance, white generals and politicians must have felt confident that the

Indian troubles of the north were at an end. Indeed, by 1877, there was scarcely a tribe in all the vast northern territories of the United States that had not been cajoled or compelled to cede their lands and go on to a reservation, where they would live under white supervision. True, there was one small tribe that was still stubbornly following its old way of life – the Lower Nez Percés – but they were few in numbers and had no history of armed resistance. As a matter of fact, twice earlier in the century, in 1849 and again in 1858, when some of the plateau tribes had struck at the settlers swarming through their country along the Oregon trail, the Nez Percés had remained friendly to white men and even offered them assistance. It was their claim that in seventy years of contact between the races, they had never shed a drop of white man's blood.

It should be explained that the Nez Percés, although they considered themselves to be one people, were made up of several confederated bands. Broadly speaking, they could be divided into two groups: the Upper Nez Percés, who lived along the Clearwater River in what is now Idaho, and the Lower Nez Percés, whose territory was in north-east Oregon. The home range of the Lower Nez Percés was an area bounded in the west by the majestic Blue Mountains, and in the east by the rushing waters of the Snake River. Much of the country in between was harsh and rugged. It was cut by two river valleys, the better of which, the Wallowa valley, was considered by the Lower Nez Percés to be their heartland. It was a place they held in deep affection.

overleaf: the Nez Percé heartland, the Wallowa valley

Already, by 1860, gold had been found at Orofino on the Clearwater and other strikes were soon to follow. Miners flocked into the north-west, men out to get rich quick, who had little patience with the Indians they found living there. In view of this situation, the government made a determined effort to drive the Indians of the region on to reservations, so as to avert future trouble. In 1863 a treaty was offered to both branches of the Nez Percés. Its terms were accepted by the Upper Nez Percés, who entered the reservation set aside for the tribe at Lapwai. The Lower Nez Percés did not prove so accommodating.

At this time, the leader of the Lower Nez Percés was not the Chief Joseph who is the main subject of this story, but his father, whom white settlers called Old Joseph to differentiate him from his son. On behalf of his people, Old Joseph rejected the proposal that they should give up their territory and move to Lapwai. He called it a "thief treaty" and never recognized its terms. Like his son, Old Joseph was a shrewd man. He guessed that trickery might now be employed to trap his people, and warned them in future not to accept so much as a blanket from white men. "If you do," he told them, "after a while they will claim that you have taken pay for your country."

In 1871, when Old Joseph died, the Lower Nez Percés were still hanging on to their ancestral lands but the pressures were growing on them all the time. When Old Joseph knew that he was dying, he called his son to him. Young Joseph was, at this time, a man in his thirties, tall and handsome, with courteous manners and a sharp intelligence. Here is his account of what happened between them: "I saw that he was dying and I took his hand in mine. He said, 'My son, my body is returning to my mother, the Earth, and my spirit going very soon to see the Great Spirit. When I am gone, think of your country. You are now chief of these people. They look to you to guide them. Always remember, your father never sold his country. Stop your ears when you are asked to sign a treaty. A few years more and the white men will be all round you. They have their eyes on this land. Do not forget my dying words. This country holds your father's body: never sell the bones of your father and mother.' I pressed my father's hand," Joseph goes on, "and I told him I would guard his grave with my life . . . I buried him at Wallowa, the valley of the Winding Waters. I love that land more than all the rest of the world. A man who would not honour his father's grave is worse than a wild animal."

In the years that followed Old Joseph's death, as he had foreseen, the pressures mounted upon his son. Gold was found in the neighbouring mountains and this attracted more white men, some of whom helped themselves to Nez Percé horses and ran off with their cattle. Chief Joseph said of these thieves: "They stole a great many horses, and we could not get them back because we were Indians. They drove away our cattle, and branded our young calves. The white men told lies for each other, and we could do nothing. We had no friend to plead our case in the law-councils."

Despite all this, Joseph managed to persuade his

young men not to strike back at the whites. He knew what the outcome of that would be. Soon after Joseph became chief, one of his tribe was murdered by settlers, and though Joseph did not seek revenge in the tradi- tional Indian way, by killing a white man in return, he did begin to demand from that moment on that all settlers should be made to leave the country of the Nez Percés. He kept demanding this for some years, without success.

Perhaps because he had made such a demand, government officials came to see Joseph in 1872, and tried to get him to agree to take his people out of the Wallowa valley and on to the reservation at Lapwai. Joseph's first response was a defiant one. "We will," he declared, "defend this land as long as a drop of Indian blood runs in the hearts of our young men." On reflection, he decided his best chance lay in an appeal to the highest authority in America. He therefore sent an appeal to the President of the U.S., Ulysses Grant, asking him to let his people stay on the land where they had always lived. In June 1873 President Grant sent his answer. He decided in favour of Chief Joseph, and issued an order that meant the Wallowa valley was no longer open to further settlement by white men. Chief Joseph must have felt the same sort of relief as the Sioux had done when they were promised the Black Hills and the Powder River Country "forever". There was more hope of the Nez Percés being left in possession of Wallowa. It was not a rich or splendid land like the Powder River Country, and had little to recommend it from the white point of view, as a report written by

In 1872, Chief Joseph still hoped for a peace- ful solution to the resettlement problem

Captain Whipple in 1875 makes clear. "The Wallowa valley," wrote Whipple, "is only fit for stock-raising, and not really for that because of the long winters. It must be borne in mind that Indian horses will live through winters where the white man's cattle would perish." Captain Whipple went on to remark dryly that "the average American is not, as a rule, slow to take advantage of openings to secure land claims which may become valuable later, but few of them seem to locate claims in the Wallowa valley . . . This shows how the white people regard the valley. The Indians, on the other hand, love it." It was this love which would lead them into war.

During the early years of the 1870s, white settlers went on making trouble with the Nez Percés, but as before, Joseph managed to hold his people in check. Then, in 1875, the President changed his mind about the Wallowa valley, and it was officially opened again to white settlement. From that time on, things were bound to grow worse between the settlers and the Nez Percés, and they did. Another Indian was killed in 1875, and in August of the same year, a settler called Henry Mason seized two Nez Percés and gave them a brutal whipping. Joseph's words about the failure of the Nez Percés to get justice at the law-councils seem to be borne out by what happened in this instance. As he knew who had done the whipping, Joseph felt able to take the case to law. His complaint was judged by a "council of arbitration" made up of three white men – it was dismissed out of hand. Then, in June 1876, a white man called Finlay committed a worse outrage, actually killing a brother of Chief Joseph. Even in face of such provocation, Joseph persuaded his people not to seek revenge. He simply kept on telling the authorities that he wanted all the settlers to leave his land. But by this time, it was not the white men who were in danger of being forced to leave – it was Joseph and the Nez Percés.

In 1876 the government set up a commission to decide whether Joseph and his people should be moved on to a reservation. This commission met in the mission-church at Lapwai and called Joseph and the lesser chiefs of the Nez Percés to come before it. The commissioners included the somewhat ominous presence of General Howard, military commander of the Columbia district. The Indian party, besides Joseph and his brother Ollicut, included such warriors as Looking Glass and an old man called Too-hool-hoolzote, who was a person of some importance among the Nez Percés. As we have seen, all the Indian tribes held mystical beliefs, but Too-hool-hoolzote was a prophet and seer of a new kind. He preached doctrines that were becoming more important among Indians generally, now that their land was being taken away and their way of life changed. Too-hool-hoolzote's views about the nature of land and its treatment were like those of Chief Joseph and other Indians. He argued that the earth should never be divided up. It should not be cut with the plough nor should the fruits of the earth be forced from it by farming. But he also proclaimed a new message, a message of forlorn hope, born out of despair. Too-hool-hoolzote said that very soon an

Indian saviour would appear from the east, a saviour who would banish the white men from Indian lands, call back the Indian dead, and bring about the return of the buffalo, so that Indians would find themselves living once more as they had done in the old days before the appearance of the whites. White observers called Too-hool-hoolzote's religion the "Drummer-Dreamer" cult. Other cults like it were to spring up among the dispossessed Indians, the most famous of them being the Dance of the Ghosts, which was to end in the massacre of Wounded Knee in 1890.

Beliefs like those held by Too-hool-hoolzote were naturally unpopular among the missionaries, who had an important influence on government thinking. The missionaries were anxious to make Christians of all Indians as soon as possible. The need to do this was one of the factors weighed by the Commissioners in coming to their decision about Joseph's people. In fact, it was urged by a certain churchman that the Nez Percés should "be brought within the Christianizing influence of the reservation – by force if necessary." That last phrase sounds less than Christian today, but seems to have been quite acceptable then.

Joseph acted as spokesman for his people, impressing the Commissioners by his eloquent arguments, which they called his "dexterity at intellectual fencing". "God," said Joseph, "when he created the earth did not make any marks on it, or any lines of division or separation – and the earth should be left as God made it." Joseph went on to tell the Commissioners that he looked on the land as a man looked on

Ollicut, Joseph's much loved younger brother

his mother. The land meant too much to his heart for him ever to sell it for silver or gold. He thought it wrong to abuse the land. He and his people were content to live on the natural fruits it gave them. Joseph replied to the white man's offer of compensation by saying he asked for nothing from the President. He and his people were able to look after themselves. They did not need help; they did not need money. They asked only to be left alone in their own country at Wallowa. The Commissioners raised the idea of making Wallowa into a reservation but Joseph refused. "We do not want Wallowa as a reservation," he told them. "If that were to happen, I and my people would have to bow to the will of other men. We would lose our independence, and be forced to obey laws not of our own making."

Despite Joseph's arguments, the Commissioners recommended that the Nez Percés should be ordered on to the reservation at Lapwai. They were not happy with the idea of any Indians remaining outside direct white control. They pointed to the growth of heathen sects among the Nez Percés, and in particular the Drummer-Dreamers, which they saw as a bad sign. The Commissioners also suggested that if the Lower Nez Percés were allowed to go on with their roving style of life, it would only lead to discontent among other Indians who by now were committed to reservations and forbidden to leave them without the consent of the government Agent. The Commissioners were particularly disturbed by Joseph's remarks that he and his people did not want to lose their freedom to go from one place to another – which meant above all, their right to travel through lands occupied by whites, across the Rocky Mountains to the Powder River country for the buffalo-hunt. The Commissioners felt this custom could not go on. It was unsettling to the other tribes, who might well feel envious and regret their treaties, and it was dangerous in itself, as sooner or later it was sure to lead to clashes between the growing white population and the Indians still following their old hunting trails.

For their own good, this last band of roving Indians must be put on a reservation, taught to till the soil, and instructed in Christianity. As Captain Whipple, a man with sympathy for the Indians, remarked: "The Nez Percés realize that once they go to the Lapwai reservation, or one similar, they will be forced to give up their horse herds, which are their main wealth, and that as a community they will cease to exist." Lines of "division and separation" would be made in the earth of the reservation, each household being given twenty or thirty acres of land to work, but the horses which were their pride could not be kept in such circumstances and would have to be given up. The buffalo-hunts would be forbidden. These new ways would tear the ties of kinship asunder.

The Commission, and later, the United States government, saw it as natural and inevitable that the Nez Percés should be placed on a reservation. They argued that they were acting for the good of the Indians and went on to prove – to their own satisfaction – that the whites already had a right to Wallowa and the surrounding country. They used some very dubious legal arguments and, having justified themselves in this way, the officials were able, with a clear conscience, to order General Howard to arrange for the removal of Joseph's people to the reservation at Lapwai. If the Indians would not go of their own free will, General Howard was given the power to use soldiers against them. In private, General Howard had already said that it would be "a great mistake to take from Joseph and his band of Nez Percés that (Wallowa) valley", but as a serving officer he had to obey the orders he was given. Howard called Joseph and the other chiefs to hear the decision of the government. He told them briskly that they had thirty days, up to 14 May 1877, in which to clear the land of their herds and move on to Lapwai reservation. Breaking the news cannot have been a pleasant task for Howard. It was perhaps his uneasy conscience that led him to act as high-handedly as he did. Some of the Indians naturally challenged the justice of this decision. In particular, Too-hool-hoolzote, the leader of the Drummer-Dreamers, showed his defiance. He, not Joseph, was acting as spokesman for the Indians on this occasion, and he did not see much use for tact or diplomacy when none had been shown by the other side. Too-hool-hoolzote stood up and challenged the right of the white men to divide the land. "The earth is part of our body," he declared. "We cannot give it up."

General Howard gave the Nez Percés just thirty days to move on to the Lapwai reservation

This seems to have irritated General Howard, who told the Indian that he wanted to hear no more such talk. Too-hool-hoolzote then asked him this question: "Who is it can tell me what I must do and not do in my

own country?" Howard's only answer was that they would have to go. Too-hool-hoolzote said that other people could do as they liked but he, for one, was not going to live on any reservation. At this, Howard's fraying temper snapped, and he gave way to a show of power which was meant no doubt to cow the other Indians. He ordered Too-hool-hoolzote to be arrested and thrown into the guardhouse cells. As he was dragged away, struggling, Too-hool-hoolzote shouted a final mocking question at Howard: "Are you trying to scare me by bullying my body?" Howard waved the soldiers on. Too-hool-hoolzote was hustled out of the meeting, still fighting, and thrown into the lock-up.

In the stunned silence that followed the arrest of Too-hool-hoolzote, Chief Joseph took over the role of spokesman. He asked only that they be given more time to move their herds, as thirty days was too short a period, with their stock scattered and the Snake River in spring flood. Howard suspected that this was merely a delaying tactic, and answered that there could be no extension of the time limit. He warned the Nez Percés that if they were not gone in thirty days, the soldiers would come and drive them to Lapwai at gunpoint and, what was more, any cattle and horses not moved on to reservation lands by then might be seized by white men.

Joseph could see nothing for it but to agree. As he said later: "The white men were many and I knew we could not hold our own with them. We were like deer. They were like grizzly bears. We had only a small country. Their country was large. We were happy to let things remain as the Great Spirit had made them, but they were not. They would change the rivers and the mountains if they did not suit them." At a council of his warriors, Joseph still advised against resistance. "Rather than have war," he said later, "I decided I would give up my country. I would give up my father's grave; give up everything."

He was wise enough to know what the outcome of a war against the United States army must be, and in order to preserve his people, he was driven to plead for obedience to Washington, though he did so with a heavy heart. His advice was accepted at the tribal council, but as time went by and the end of the thirty days' grace drew near, some men began to gather in groups and mutter about resistance.

Even so, the trek towards Lapwai reservation was begun, but as Joseph had foreseen, the Snake river was swollen by melted snow from the mountains and proved hard to cross. The Indians had to float their women and children across the swirling water on rafts made from buffalo hides, and when they tried to swim their stock over, many animals were carried away by the torrent. Others seem to have been stolen by white men who took advantage of the general confusion to do some rustling.

The angry feelings among Joseph's warriors were hardening, and they demanded another council, even at this late stage, to decide whether or not to go on with the evacuation. At the council, White Bird showed signs of leaning towards resistance. Too-hool-hoolzote, who by this time had been set free, was quite openly in favour of fighting. He said he had personal reasons for war, and told the warriors that, so far as he was concerned, only blood could wipe out the disgrace of his imprisonment. Once more, Joseph argued against fighting. "It is better to live at peace," he told them "than to begin a war and then lie dead." But this time, in spite of the respect in which Joseph was held, some warriors began to say openly that he was a coward. In fact, Joseph was losing control of his young men. It must have seemed to them that they had nothing left to lose by fighting. Joseph knew better. He was aware that resistance might lead to the destruction of his entire people, but it was not the Indian way to accept insults meekly. The young warriors did not see why they should let themselves be driven from their ancestral lands without any attempt to defend themselves. A group of hot-blooded young Nez Percés gathered at Rocky Canyon and decided to make a fight of it. There was some argument amongst them as to what they should do. One group simply wanted to take on the soldiers, who would certainly be sent to drive them off their land if they lingered. Another group urged that they should strike without warning at the white settlers, because it was the settlers whose greed was at the root of all the troubles of the Nez Percés.

It was a dark night when a few warriors slipped out of camp, determined to take matters into their own hands, and have their revenge on the white settlers. By the next morning, four white men lay dead. The Nez Percés, the "good" Indians, who never before, in seventy years, had raised their hand against white men, were now guilty of murder. The war-party rode back to the Camas Prairie where the main body of Indians lay encamped, and went prancing their horses among the tepees, showing off the spoils they had taken from the slaughtered whites, and calling on all true warriors to join them. As it happened, Joseph and his brother Ollicut had moved their tepees away from the camp because Joseph's wife was sick. In his absence, the most senior Indian present was White Bird, who was soon swayed by the taunts and appeals of the war-party. His reaction was the traditional one for an Indian warrior. He mounted his horse and rode through the camp shouting, "There is blood. We must all join with these young men now." Soon afterwards, a war-party of about twenty braves went across the Salmon river to hunt out more white victims. They killed eight settlers, amongst them Henry Mason, the man who had dealt out the whippings the year before. Yet another war-party attacked a wagonload of ranchers who had heard the bad news, and were trying to get away to the safety of Mount Idaho. The Nez Percés left three of them dead.

There was no going back now and Chief Joseph knew it. He realized that there would be no forgiveness for these murders. The soldiers would certainly be unleashed against his people. Joseph might still have taken all those who could be persuaded to follow him on to the reservation, but that would have meant abandoning some of his young men to the soldiers. He could not find it in his heart to do that. His hand had been forced by the killings, and he decided on war. He put himself in charge of operations, although he had deep forebodings about the outcome. As he was to say later: "I would have given my own life if that would have undone the killing of white men by my people. I blame my young men, but I also blame the white settlers."

Chief Joseph's first idea was to lead his people over the mountains towards the Powder River Country, and perhaps he was already thinking that the best hope for the Nez Percés would be to follow Sitting Bull's example and flee across the border into Canada. "I meant to take my people over to the buffalo country," Joseph said later. "Take them without fighting, if possible. We moved first to White Bird Canyon and camped there. We meant to round up our stock and then leave."

They did not get the chance to leave. Already, by 16 May, the first column of soldiers had been sent to seek them out and punish them. Colonel Perry came marching down from Fort Lapwai with a force of about a hundred soldiers and a few civilian volunteers. It was not a large force but General Howard must have decided to employ speed rather than numbers, thinking that a hundred regular troops would be enough to break a tribe like the Nez Percés which was inexperienced in war and did not yet have the reputation it was soon to gain. The decision must have seemed a reasonable one at the time. As Perry and his troopers pushed south, Chief Joseph took over command of the Nez Percé fighting men. The war between Joseph's people and the armies of the United States had begun.

overleaf: this map shows the route taken by Chief Joseph and his tribe on their long trek across the mountains towards Canada, and the routes of pursuit of Colonel Miles, Colonel Gibbon and Colonel Sturgis as they tried to intercept the Indian party. General Howard's route is not shown separately – he followed close on the heels of the Nez Percés

opposite: Nez Percé babies were placed on cradleboards and could be carried on their mothers' backs

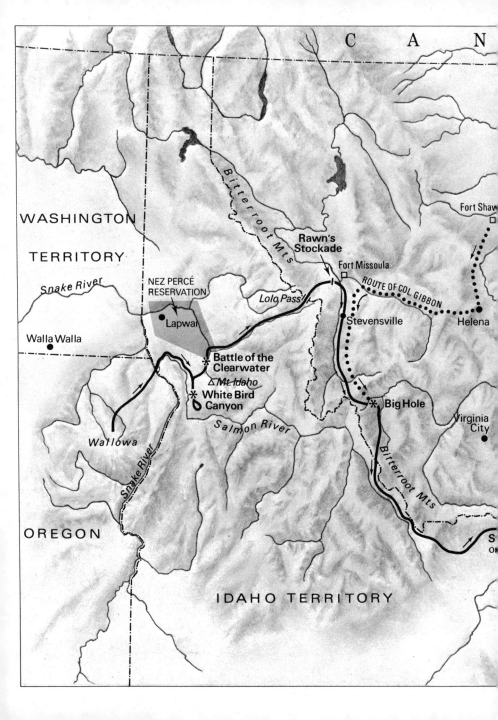

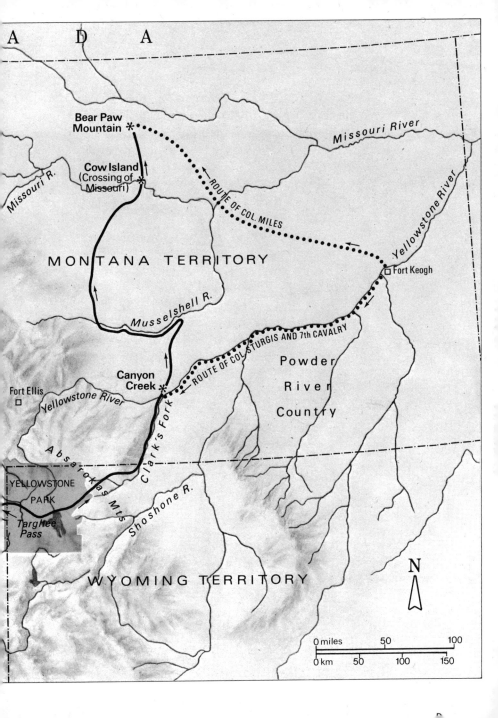

C A N A D A

Bear Paw
Mountain *

Missouri River

Cow Island
(Crossing of
Missouri)

Missouri R.

ROUTE OF COL. MILES

MONTANA TERRITORY

Yellowstone River

Fort Keogh

Musselshell R.

ROUTE OF COL. STURGIS AND 7th CAVALRY

Powder

River

Country

Canyon
Creek *

Clark's Fork

Fort Ellis

Yellowstone River

Absarokas Mts

YELLOWSTONE
PARK

Targhee
Pass

Shoshone R.

WYOMING TERRITORY

N

0 miles   50   100
0 km   50   100   150

Joseph's tactics were to lure the soldiers into White Bird canyon and ambush them there. He managed this successfully. The main body of the Nez Percés engaged the unsuspecting enemy, pouring volleys at them suddenly from behind boulders and makeshift barricades of stones. Meanwhile, another group of Indians was sent along the top of the hills to cut off the escape route of Perry's men. Seeing they were in danger of being trapped, the soldiers broke and ran headlong. Some of them managed to get to the head of the canyon before the encircling party of Nez Percés arrived, but later ones, finding their way already barred, turned aside up a narrow ravine, hoping to make good their escape that way. They suffered badly. The climb was steep, the ground treacherous, and as they struggled upwards, they were raked by accurate fire from Indian sharpshooters. To complete the rout, Nez Percé horsemen chased the fleeing cavalry twelve miles across country, harrying them to within a short distance of Mount Idaho. Of the hundred soldiers who had ridden into White Bird canyon that morning, only sixty-five remained alive at nightfall, and some of them were wounded. Joseph had fought his first battle and won a surprisingly dramatic victory. He had also captured a number of army rifles and a good supply of ammunition.

When the bad news was brought to General Howard, he immediately ordered larger numbers of troops to take the field against the Nez Percés, but Chief Joseph eluded them, leading his people away by devious routes through mountainous country. The one reconnaissance party that managed to get close to the Nez Percés was attacked, and all twelve members of it killed. General Howard found himself being tricked and out-manoeuvred by Joseph who was proving to be a clever strategist, even though he had never fought a campaign before. The situation was a humiliating one for General Howard, who knew how shocked the people of the United States had been only the previous year by the defeat of Custer at the Little Big Horn. Now, once again, the reputation of the Army was being challenged, this time by a petty band of hostile Indians with nothing like the military strength of the Sioux. Howard pushed doggedly after the Nez Percés, determined to corner them and smash them, once and for all.

By now, Joseph had led his people to the Clearwater river, where he was joined by his friend, Chief Looking Glass, who had succeeded in dodging the contingent of troops sent to arrest him and his band. Looking Glass's people had been forced to abandon over seven hundred horses in making good their escape but the troops had not managed to capture a single Indian. News came to Joseph that Howard's army was approaching fast, and he decided to stand and fight. For safety's sake, Joseph placed his camp, with the women and children and the old people, over on the far side of the Clearwater River. He and his warriors took up a position on the near side and waited for Howard to advance. In terms of numbers, the odds were against Joseph's men this time. Even with the reinforcements brought by Looking Glass, the Nez Percés could not

overleaf:
The Nez Percés, joined by Chief Looking Glass and his band, made camp on the banks of the Clearwater River, and for five days were able to regather their strength before facing General Howard and his men

51

muster so many as three hundred warriors, though some of the young squaws did help their menfolk in the fighting. This was the entire military strength of the Nez Percés. There were no more reserves on which to draw. These warriors, together with some five or six hundred non-combatants across the river, made up the entire "nation" of the Nez Percés. It was a pitifully small group to take on the military might of the United States, and one in which every casualty was deeply felt. The members of the tribe all knew each other, all of them felt the loss of each man, and they knew that every death opened a gap in their ranks that could never be filled again.

General Howard rode at the head of four hundred regular troops, backed up by numerous teamsters and baggage-men. His advantage was not only one of numbers. He had brought with him weapons which the Nez Percés could not match – notably a field howitzer and a couple of Gatling guns. And of course, any casualties among Howard's army could easily be replaced. There was an endless supply of white soldiers. In fact, at that moment, other columns were being fitted out further East, ready to march against Joseph, if need be.

On the afternoon of 11 June 1877, Howard's troops clashed with Joseph's warriors on the bank of the Clearwater River. Despite his superiority in numbers, Howard could not break through the Indian defences. His charges were rolled back, and when night fell on the battle-field it found the Nez Percés still holding their positions. Next morning the fighting began in earnest again and went on through several more hot and bloody hours. Howard must have been astonished and angered by the stubborn resistance of the Nez Percés, but he knew something that Joseph could not know: reinforcements were on their way to him. On the afternoon of 12 June, after twenty-four hours of fighting, Joseph's tired warriors saw a cloud of dust approaching. It was the fresh column of U.S. cavalry that Howard had been expecting. The column was sent into immediate action. It punched hard at the Indian flank, which began to wilt under the assault. The moment was a desperate one for Joseph. He had to order the immediate withdrawal of his warriors across the river. The Nez Percés pulled back success-fully, but the Army howitzer was brought up very fast, and trained on the Indian camp before the tents could be struck. Shells were bursting in the camp while women were still struggling to take down the heavy hide tepees. Amidst the confusion, Joseph had to organize a rearguard, and also to oversee the retreat of the non-combatants and ensure that the vital horse-herds were driven safely away. In order to deter Howard's troops from pressing home their advantage, Joseph sent a large body of Nez Percé horsemen to hang on the right front of the enemy and threaten attack. This tactic succeeded in buying Joseph time. Howard ordered his men to stand where they were and see to their defences. Meanwhile, Joseph's people streamed away in full flight. When the main body of Nez Percés had made good their escape, the mounted warriors drew off without a fight, and rode quickly

away, too. Once more, Chief Joseph had shown the quality of his leadership. He had got his people out of a desperate situation, and denied Howard the decisive victory he so much wanted. This battle also serves to highlight an important difference between Joseph's position as a leader, and that of a general like Howard. Joseph was not simply in command of a fighting force, he was also the guardian of a people. He had always to bear in mind the safety of the children, the sick, and the old. General Howard had no such worries. His was an army, made up of professional soldiers, with no dependants near at hand.

The Nez Percés tramped away into the mountains and when Howard sent an advance column against them, it was ambushed and badly mauled. After that, Howard's forces advanced more cautiously so that although the Nez Percés had children and old people in their ranks, they were able to outdistance the soldiers. By the next night, Joseph's people were encamped in an almost impregnable position at the entrance to the Lolo trail. This was the trail which in happier days the Nez Percé hunters had taken on their way to the great buffalo *illahu* in the Powder River country. It was a notoriously bad trail. To cross it meant struggling along dizzy paths, up the sides of mountains amongst rocks and treacherous screes, clambering over fallen timber, crossing fierce torrents. General Sherman said of it: "The Lolo trail is universally admitted by all who have travelled on it, from Lewis and Clarke on, as one of the worst trails for both man and beast on this continent." Joseph led his

Nez Percé woman in handsomely beaded costume

people and their herds safely over it, across the Bitter-root Mountains. It was another great feat of leadership on his part, but one that must have called for a great deal of courage and endurance from the weaker members of the tribe as they struggled to keep up.

The Nez Percés must have felt that by this arduous crossing they had moved out of danger. They had left General Howard and his heavily laden baggage trains far behind and successfully reached Montana terri-tory, but to their disappointment and dismay, they were once again met by soldiers. It must have seemed to them that no matter what they did, they could not keep the advantages they won. In fact, the telegraph, the new invention of the white man, was working against them. By means of this, troops could be alerted, and columns set in motion, with a speed that would have been unthinkable in earlier times.

Chief Joseph saw that the soldiers were building a barricade of logs across a narrow place in the trail. He, White Bird and Looking Glass rode down under a flag of truce to talk with Captain Rawn, the officer in command. "We are going through here without fighting, if you will let us," Joseph told Rawn. "But we are going through, anyhow."

Chief Joseph at-tempted to shake off General Howard by leading his people over the Lolo Trail. 150 miles long, it led over the Bitterroot Mountains, and was a notoriously difficult route

Captain Rawn, with the advantage of the telegraph, knew that not only was General Howard pursuing Joseph's people from the West but another large force under Colonel Gibbon was advancing towards them from the East. In these circumstances, Rawn decided his best move was to play for time. He managed to stretch out his talks with the Indian leaders for two

days before Joseph declared that they could wait no longer. Joseph had realized how expensive it would be in terms of lives for his warriors to have to mount a frontal attack on the barricade so he had sent out scouts to find a route up the mountains that would take them round it. At dawn on 28 July, Looking Glass led the main body of Nez Percé warriors out on to the slopes of the canyon and formed them into a screening line. Captain Rawn's attention was naturally drawn towards this large enemy force, which looked as if it might be going to cause trouble. Meanwhile, Joseph and the rest of his warriors were shepherding the women, children, and the old people, together with the horse-herds, up a gulch which took them to the top of the mountain. From there, they were able to by-pass the barricade and join the trail further along. Once this had been done, Looking Glass and his warriors melted away and followed the rest of Joseph's people over the mountain route. Eventually, Rawn realized he had been tricked and went after the Nez Percés, but a couple of skirmishes with the Indian rear-guard persuaded him that his best plan was to fall back on his barricade. Once more, Chief Joseph had out-witted his opponents.

Knowing his people were weary, and in need of fresh game, Joseph headed south into the Big Hole country. By now, he may have even been hoping that the soldiers would have become discouraged by their lack of success and would leave the Nez Percés alone, in which case the long and dangerous march to Canada would not need to be made. If Chief Joseph did harbour any such hopes, they were about to be dashed. Unknown to Joseph, Colonel Gibbon had been marching from Helena, in Montana, at the head of about two hundred cavalrymen and some local volunteers. He also had artillery in the shape of a howitzer. Gibbon had meant to intercept the Nez Percés but this plan failed because of Joseph's unexpected move south into the Big Hole country. Now he followed the Nez Percé trail and on 8 August his scouts reported that they had spotted the Indians, camped on the bank of the Big Hole River. All through that afternoon, Gibbon stealthily deployed his men on a wooded hill-slope overlooking the Nez Percé encampment. Gibbon decided to mount the usual surprise attack at dawn next day, and he let it be known that this was not an occasion when he would insist on prisoners being taken, male or female.

Joseph's people were resting with no suspicion of danger. They knew they had left Howard far behind, and did not guess that yet another force of soldiers had been sent against them. At first light on 9 August, Gibbon gave the signal, and his soldiers began firing volleys into the sleeping camp. Bullets ripped through the tepees. Some people were killed in their tents, others shot down as they ran outside. There was great confusion. Gibbon gave the order for his soldiers to charge into the camp and complete their work of destruction. The Indians fled, apparently in hopeless panic, leaving their dead and wounded behind. No prisoners were taken by Gibbon's men. Those Indians still alive were finished off either with bullets from close quarters or by the stocks of guns and the heels of boots. It looked as if this time the Nez Percé cause was lost, but already their leaders were rallying them. Chief Joseph and White Bird led a counter-attack so furious that it swept Gibbon and his troops right out of the occupied camp. As they fell back in disorder, it was suddenly the soldiers who were in danger of being overwhelmed. They retreated to a wooded spur, which they defended desperately, throwing up rough timber barricades and cutting shallow trenches, but their position must have seemed hopeless. The Nez Percés had them completely encircled and pinned down. Their commanding officer, Colonel Gibbon, had been wounded in the retreat. Their howitzer had fallen into the hands of Joseph's warriors, who set about wrecking the hated weapon. All that day a number of Nez Percés besieged the soldiers, whilst Joseph organized the salvaging of the Indian camp and the movement of the main body of his people out of harm's way. It is quite likely that Gibbon's force would have been starved out and killed by the furious Nez Percé warriors, but by now General Howard was coming into striking distance and he sent a troop of cavalry to Gibbon's assistance. When the Nez Percé besiegers saw them, they galloped away and brought Joseph the dispiriting news that General Howard was once more on their heels. Behind them they left thirty dead troopers, and fifty more wounded.

Although this action ended in yet another forced march by the Nez Percés, they had managed to retain their freedom by a brilliant stroke of arms, turning what had looked like certain defeat into another victory. But the cost had been high. Joseph's people left more than eighty dead on the banks of the Big Hole River, fifty of them women and children. Howard's column joined forces with Gibbon's troops on the field of battle and Howard's Bannock Indian scouts were allowed to scalp and mutilate the Nez Percé dead, with white men standing by and raising no objection. This was in striking contrast to the conduct of the Nez Percés themselves, of whom General Sherman was to write: "The Nez Percés abstained from scalping, let captive white women go free, and did not commit indiscriminate murder of peaceful families, which was usual."

It was essential that Joseph and his people should put some distance between themselves and General Howard's troops, who soon took up the pursuit. "We retreated as quickly as we could," Joseph said later. "After six days, General Howard came close to us, and we went out and captured a lot of his mules and horses." This stock raid was a very dashing affair. The Nez Percé horsemen fooled Howard's sentries by riding up at dusk in column of fours, advancing regularly and without haste. The guards thought it could only be a squadron of their own cavalry approaching, and failed to raise the alarm until the Nez Percé warriors had got very close to them. The Indians succeeded in driving off a large number of horses and mules, though there were enough mounts left in Howard's camp for him to order three companies of cavalry into the saddle to pursue the raiders and get back the stolen beasts. The soldiers did manage to retrieve about fifty horses, but then amazingly, the Nez Percés had the nerve to strike again and made off with most of those that had been recovered. At the end of that daring night's work, Howard's column was stripped of many of its pack animals, which allowed the Nez Percés to make good their escape yet again, while Howard waited for new supplies of horses and mules to reach him from Virginia City.

Joseph now led his weary people through the Targhee (Tacher's) Pass into Yellowstone Park. This beautiful area had been declared a National Park by the United States government some five years earlier. Perhaps no other circumstance in the Nez Percés flight is more movingly symbolic than that this last band of free Indians should find themselves travelling through an area that had already been designated as a pleasure-ground for white tourists. They marched through more open country to the region of geysers, hot springs, and sulphur lands, unaware as yet that still another column was advancing against them. A detachment of the Seventh Cavalry, back at full strength after the Custer disaster, had been dispatched towards the Yellowstone. The soldiers pushed forward, eager to take revenge, and restore their regimental honour.

By clever manoeuvring, Chief Joseph once more outwitted his pursuers. Colonel Sturgis, who led the new column, was deceived into blocking the trail down Stinking Water whilst Joseph's people slipped through a narrow canyon to Clark's Fork and from there went down to the Yellowstone again. Realizing his mistake,

Sturgis set off in pursuit of the Nez Percés, and caught up with the weary fugitives on the alkaline sage-brush plains across the Yellowstone River. Again, the Indian rearguard managed to hold off the soldiers long enough to let their people reach the entrance to a narrow valley called Canyon Creek, which provided them with some defence. Unfortunately, they had to abandon four hundred ponies in their retreat. Sturgis sent his troops up the valley but the Nez Percés brought off a fighting withdrawal, though five hundred more of their horses were lost. They shook loose of Sturgis and retreated fast up the Mussel Shell River, with Chief Joseph definitely heading for Canada now. It was obvious to him that the soldiers would never stop chasing his people, so their only hope must be to seek refuge, like Sitting Bull, in Canada.

The Nez Percés force-marched round the Judith Mountains, and reached the Missouri river at Cow Island on 23 September. They knew that soldiers were still following them but reckoned they had at least a couple of days in hand. They could not be aware that yet another powerful column of troops under Colonel "Bear-Coat" Miles had been ordered from Fort Keogh to strike swiftly across country and cut off their retreat. Joseph led his people over the Missouri and north towards the Canadian border, where they found themselves passing through a stretch of country lying around the Bear Paw and the Little Rocky mountains, which was described by a writer at that time as "a veritable Eden". The people were dropping with weariness, their ponies were worn out, and so, as the

Nez Percé scouts had seen no sign of enemy forces in the last three days, Chief Joseph decided he could risk calling a day's halt. There were buffalo still surviving in this area, and Joseph knew their meat would strengthen his people on their last dash to the Canadian border, now little more than thirty miles away. The spirits of the Nez Percés must have risen as they took their rest at the camp on Bear Paw Mountain, but the short delay they made was to prove fatal.

Next morning, before they had time to strike camp, the alarm was raised by two of their scouts. A different detachment of soldiers was advancing on them from the east, and coming up fast. "Bear Coat" Miles had succeeded in finding Joseph's people before they could reach the border. Miles now ordered a cavalry charge and the troopers galloped forward, six hundred strong. The Nez Percés had just enough time for their non-combatants to gain the cover of the ravines running down from the bluffs. The warriors stood firm in the camp, and as the first wave of soldiers swept down on them, they struck back with a withering volley of fire. The charge faltered and stopped in a chaos of falling men and horses. The Nez Percés now pressed forward against the disorganized enemy. "We fought at close range," said Joseph. "Not more than twenty steps apart. We drove the soldiers back and captured arms and ammunition from them." The charge was rolled back, but only at the cost of further grievous losses to the Nez Percés. In this fight, twenty-seven more of their men were killed and three of their young women. Among the dead were Joseph's brother, Ollicut, and

Colonel Miles, with infantry and cavalry, set out from Fort Keogh. He intercepted the Nez Percés at their camp in the Bear Paw Mountains

the tough old prophet, Too-hool-hoolzote.

That night, under cover of darkness, Joseph and his people tried to slip away towards Canada, but the road was barred. Miles had them surrounded. The Nez Percé warriors dug in and made ready to meet another onslaught, but none came. Miles had suffered sufficient casualties among his troops to make him wary of mounting another frontal attack. Besides, there was no reason to do so. He had the Indians trapped. The Nez Percés were harassed by sniping and skirmishing, and every now and then a shell was lobbed into their positions. Among the ravines, the Nez Percés were also suffering from the cold. The weather was breaking. Their last fight had been conducted among flurries of snow. The hard northern winter was coming down. At night, the chill was bitter. In these circumstances, Miles could afford to wait, particularly as he knew that General Howard's army would soon be arriving from the south.

Chief Joseph sent messengers to try to find Sitting Bull and appeal to him for help, but it does not seem that any of the messengers got through. When General Howard's column came trundling into view to reinforce Miles, Chief Joseph must have been forced to the bitter realization that this time there could be no escape. After the Nez Percés had endured four days of siege, Joseph agreed to come down under a flag of truce and receive the terms of surrender proposed by the American officers. "Bear-Coat" Miles gave Joseph an assurance that if his people laid down their arms, their lives would be spared, and they would be allowed to join their kinsfolk on the reservation at Lapwai.

Joseph took these promises back to his besieged tribe, and called a council of warriors to find out how they felt about accepting the terms. Opinion was divided. Looking Glass and White Bird were among those who wanted to go on with the fight. They were so close to Canada that they must have felt one last effort might get them there. Joseph postponed a decision until next day. By that time, Looking Glass was dead, his skull shattered by a sniper's bullet. White Bird still urged making a break for it but Joseph had weighed up the situation, and come to the conclusion that, as chief of the tribe, he could not agree with White Bird. He had to consider all his people, not only the able-bodied. As he put it himself: "We could have escaped from Bear Paw Mountain, but only if we had left behind our wounded, our old women and our children. We were not prepared to do this." He added grimly, "We have never heard of a wounded Indian recovering once he falls into the hands of white men."

Joseph's duty, as he saw it, was to stay with the weak and the helpless among his people, but there was no question of him trying to force White Bird to do the same. White Bird, unable to stomach the idea of surrender and captivity, led a band of irreconcilable Nez Percé warriors through the enemy lines on the fifth night of the siege and reached Canada successfully, where they joined Sitting Bull's band of Sioux. Next morning, Chief Joseph surrendered in the name of the bulk of his people, accepting the terms offered, which included not only the return of the Nez Percé survivors to the reservation at Lapwai but the giving back of more than a thousand horses, seized by the United States army during the course of the fighting.

Chief Joseph made a speech at the surrender ceremony which shows the dreadful state to which the Nez Percés had been reduced and reflects Joseph's despair at the plight of his people:

"I am tired of fighting. Our chiefs are all killed. Looking Glass is dead. Too-hool-hoolzote is dead. The old counsellors are dead. It is the young men who say 'yes' or 'no' now. The leader of the young men, Ollicut, is also dead. It is cold. We have no blankets. The little children are freezing to death . . . Hear me, my chiefs, I am tired; my heart is sick and sad. From where the sun now stands I will fight no more forever."

These words mark the end of all serious Indian resistance in the Northern territories of the United States. Even Sitting Bull was to come back over the border a few years later, pining for his people and his homeland, and surrender without a fight.

Sadly, the suffering of Joseph's people was not over. The promises made to Joseph were not kept. Colonel Miles had offered his terms in good faith and was afterwards to write: "I acted on what I supposed was the original design of the government to place these Indians on their own reservation, and so informed them." General Howard, too, seems to have expected to receive the Nez Percés back in his own Department, but the politicians thought otherwise. Officials decided that it would be too dangerous to send the Nez

Percés back to their own country. It was argued that if they were returned, the local settlers would "wage an unrelenting war of vengeance" on them because of the murders committed at the beginning of the outbreak. They were shipped instead to Fort Leavenworth in Kansas, which was a strange, hostile country to them; a place of swampy flats and shelterless plains, far removed in every sense from the mountains and valleys of their homeland. None of their horses was ever returned to them.

The Nez Percés did not prosper in Kansas. Inspector MacNeil, reporting on the site of the camp chosen for them at Fort Leavenworth, wrote: "It lies between a lagoon and the river, the worst possible place that could have been selected, and the sanitary condition of the Indians proves it . . . One half of them can be said to be sick, and all are affected by the poisonous malaria of the camp. Within a few months, they have lost more than a quarter of their number by sickness."

After nearly a hundred of them had died, Joseph's people were transferred to a barren plain on the Salt Fork of the Arkansas River, but this did not seem to help. In 1881, after four years of captivity, their Agent, Mr Jordan, reported that "the Nez Percés have still not become acclimatized, and this accounts for the large amount of sickness and the many deaths among them." The following year, the story was the same. Commissioner Price wrote a report on the surviving Nez Percés in which he said, "Their numbers are sadly depleted and if they stay where they are they will become virtually extinct." He went on to suggest returning them to their own people at Lapwai. Two years later, in 1884, nothing had been done about this recommendation, and their current Agent, Mr Scott, was driven to write, "The Nez Percés are extremely anxious to return to their own country. They regard themselves as exiles. Many of them have died, and there is a tinge of melancholy in their bearing and conversation that is truly pathetic. I think they should be sent back."

During all this time, Joseph had shared the sorrows of his people. At one point, liberal politicians managed to arrange for him to go to Washington to make an appeal for justice. Chief Joseph told the assembled statesmen: "I believed General Miles or I would never have surrendered." He went on to say, "I am tired of talk that comes to nothing. It makes my heart sick when I remember all the good words and broken promises. You might as well expect a river to run backwards as to expect any man born free to be content when he is penned up and denied his liberty."

At last, in the spring of 1885, the Government decided to act. One hundred and eighteen Nez Percés were allowed to rejoin their kinsfolk at Lapwai, but the rest were sent to the Colville reservation in Washington Territory. Chief Joseph was among them.

In 1889, the government sent their agent, Alice Fletcher, to Lapwai to persuade the Indians to accept individual parcels of land, rather than having the reservation wholly under tribal ownership. Chief Joseph travelled from Colville to meet her, but he would not accept land on the reservation. If he could

Government agent, Alice Fletcher, an anthropologist with great experience of Indian affairs, was sent to Lapwai in 1889 to organize land allottment. Chief Joseph travelled from Colville to see her

not return to his beloved Wallowa valley, he would remain at Colville.

In one sense, the story of Chief Joseph and the Lower Nez Percés ends here. It can be said of them that they fought the last and most heroic of the Indian wars of the north. During the summer and autumn of 1877 they marched some thirteen hundred miles, much of it over appallingly difficult country, driving themselves to feats of endurance which men could scarcely believe possible. In the course of their flight, they were endlessly harried by detachments of the United States army. Five times they were brought to battle, not counting numerous skirmishes, and never suffered a defeat before they were trapped at Bear Paw Mountain. General Sherman was to call their struggle: "The most extraordinary Indian war of which there is any record." Another man who lived through these events, J. P. Dunn, who wrote as a student of Indian affairs, gave a blacker verdict. "Taking it all in all, from the first time an Indian was kidnapped on the New England coast and sold into slavery, down to the present day, the treatment of Joseph and his Nez Percés is the worst crime the white man has perpetrated on the red man."

Chief Joseph lingered on at Colville for many years in the hope that he would be allowed finally to rejoin his own people but white officialdom never sanctioned the move and he died, still in exile, on 21 September 1904, twenty-seven years after he and his tribe had fought to preserve their land, their freedom, and their way of life.

For a long time it was common among white people to dismiss Indians like Chief Joseph rather in the way that General Sheridan had dismissed Black Kettle of the Southern Cheyennes, whom he called "a superannuated old savage". Nowadays we have begun to realize that such judgements were not only harsh, they were foolish. Let us consider why.

It was in 1867, after observing the United States army at its work of "pacifying" Black Kettle's people, the Southern Cheyenne, that Commissioner Sanborn was driven to declare: "For a mighty nation to be carrying on a war with a few straggling nomads . . . is a spectacle most humiliating, an injustice unparalleled, a national crime . . . that must, sooner or later, bring down upon us or our posterity the judgement of Heaven." Nobody listened to Sanborn. The Indian tribes were swept away, and their beliefs dismissed as barbaric survivals which must be relegated to the dustbin of history. A few men might pause briefly to salute the heroism of an Indian like Chief Joseph, but even they would admit that the destruction of the Indian way of life was inevitable. As everybody agreed, progress was irresistible, and the chief driving force of progress was the hunger for material wealth. In the name of progress, nature was brutally plundered. The lure of sudden riches had captured the imagination of white men everywhere, and only in time would it become clear that the blind arrogance of such behaviour must bring its own retribution.

Sanborn's "judgement of Heaven", as it descends on Western man, takes the form of polluted air, poisoned

lakes and streams, devastated forests, soils worked to exhaustion, and in human terms, the breakdown of family ties and the general impoverishment of the quality of life that is so often complained about in the modern cities of civilized man.

We cannot bring back the dead but we can at least admit past errors and try to learn from the wisdom of men like Chief Joseph, who for so long were thought lacking in understanding. Like all Indians, Joseph showed a deep sympathy for the natural world. His protests against the raping of the earth do not seem ridiculous today. Indeed, his belief that man must work in harmony with nature has become so painfully obvious that it is hard to imagine how men could ever have brought themselves to believe otherwise.

We have started to learn again that we must look on nature as did Chief Joseph and his people, with an understanding of our due place in the scheme of things, and with feelings of love and awe rather than aggression. In this crucial sense, though the fight put up by the Nez Percés in 1877 could have had no other outcome but military defeat, it can be said that in the long run they have gained the moral victory.

Chief Joseph was never allowed to return to Wallowa. He refused to settle at Lapwai and died in exile in 1904

Reading List

ON INDIAN LIFE AND CULTURE GENERALLY:

Indians of the Americas, J. Collier. Mentor Books, 1964.
Indians of the United States: Four Centuries of their History and Culture, C. Wissler. Doubleday, 1966
The Indian Heritage of America, A.M. Josephy Jr. Penguin, 1975
The Colourful Story of North America Indians, R.B. Hassrick. Octopus Books, 1974. Excellent for younger readers.
Time of the Indian, Ulyatt. Puffin *Explorer* series. For young readers.

ON THE PLAINS INDIANS AND THEIR LIFE-STYLE:

The Sioux: Life and Customs of a Warrior Society, R.B. Hassrick. Univ. of Oklahoma Press, 1964
Cheyenne Memories, John Stands-in-Timber and M. Liberty. Yale Univ. Press, 1967
A Closer Look at Plains Indians, C. Davis. Hamish Hamilton 1977. Useful for younger readers.
The Border and the Buffalo, J.R. Cook. Citadel Press, 1967
The Long Death: The Last Days of the Plains Indians, R.K. Andrist. Macmillan (N.Y.), 1964

ON WAR-CHIEFS AND MEDICINE-MEN:

Crazy Horse, The Strange Man of the Oglalas, M. Sandoz. Knopf, 1945
Sitting Bull: Champion of the Sioux, S. Vestal. Univ. of Oklahoma Press, 1957.
Black Elk Speaks, J. G. Neihardt. Univ. of Nebraska Press, 1961. Moving account, accessible to younger readers.
The Patriot Chiefs, A.M. Josephy Jr. Viking, 1961. Also published in the Eyre and Spottiswoode *Frontier Library*.
War Chief Joseph, H.A. Howard and D.L. McGrath. Caxton Printers, Idaho, 1941
The Ghost Dance Religion, J. Money. Am. Bureau of Ethnology Report, 1896

ON NINETEENTH CENTURY INDIAN WARS, INCLUDING THE NEZ PERCÉ WAR:

Bury My Heart at Wounded Knee, Dee Brown. Pan, 1972. Very readable account.
Massacres in the Mountains, J.P. Dunn. Valuable account by contemporary. Source of many later books. First published in America in 1880's. Republished in Eyre & Spottiswoode *Frontier Library*, 1963

ON THE NEZ PERCÉ AND CHIEF JOSEPH:

The Nez Percé Indians and the Opening of the North West, A.M. Josephy Jr. Yale Univ. Press, 1965
I Will Fight No More Forever: Chief Joseph and the Nez Percé War, M.D. Beal, Univ. of Washington Press, 1963
Yellow Wolf: His Own Story, V.L. McWhorter. Caldwell, Idaho, 1940.
An Indian's View of Indian Affairs, Interview given by Chief Joseph. First published in *North American Review*, 1879

Illustration Sources

The publishers would like to thank the following for their help with illustrations:

Idaho Department of Commerce & Development 52/53, 56
Idaho Historical Society 73
Library of Congress 40, 76
Nez Percé National Historical Park 20/21, 28/29, 59
Radio Times Hulton Picture Library 24/25
Smithsonian Institution, National Anthropological Archives 12, 32, 47
US Signal Corps, National Archives 67
Wallowa County Museum 36
Jonathan Field cover illustration